CONSTRUCTION MACHINES

CHRIS OXLADE

FIREFLY BOOKS.

A FIREFLY BOOK

Published by Firefly Books Ltd. 2018

Copyright © 2016 Quarto Publishing plc

First printing

Publisher Cataloging-in-Publication Data (U.S.)

Library of Congress Control Number: 2018935562

Library and Archives Canada Cataloguing in Publication

Oxlade, Chris, author
        Construction machines / Chris Oxlade.
ISBN 978-0-228-10111-6 (softcover)
        1. Construction equipment--Juvenile literature.
2. Earthmoving machinery--Juvenile literature. I. Title.
TH900.O95 2018   j629.225   C2018-901330-3

Published in the United States by
Firefly Books (U.S.) Inc.
P.O. Box 1338, Ellicott Station
Buffalo, New York 14205

Published in Canada by
Firefly Books Ltd.
50 Staples Avenue, Unit 1
Richmond Hill, Ontario L4B 0A7

Printed in Dongguan, China TL082018

Publisher: Maxime Boucknooghe • Art Director: Susi Martin • Editorial Director: Laura Knowles Editor: Nancy Dickmann • Design: Dave Ball • Production: Beth Sweeney

Acknowledgments
The publisher thanks the following agencies for their kind permission to use their images.

Key: bg = background, t = top, b = bottom, l = left, r = right, c = center.

Alamy Stock Photo: 2-3 © Paul Springett A; 7tl © imageBROKER; 10r © imageBROKER; © Agencja Fotograficzna Caro; 14-15 © Kim Karpeles; 15t © PRISMA ARCHIVO; 19cr © Oliver Förstner; 19br © Kim Karpeles; 20-21 © qaphotos.com; 22-23bg © Peter Titmuss; 22b © Richard Peel; 25t © Ryan Etter; 28b © Construction Photography; 31c © Kim Karpeles; 37bl © Horsemen; 40-41bg © Paul Springett A; 40b © P Lawrence; 43bl © Kevin Walsh. **Corbis:** 6-7 © Guenter Rossenbach/Corbis; 21t David McNew, 22t © Robert Garvey. **Press Association:** 18-19 John Stillwell. **Shutterstock:** front cover: dragunov; back cover: tl PL, tr Richard Thornton, bl Bullstar, br vallefrias; 1 Smileus; 4-5 Rob Wilson; 4b Krivosheev Vitaly; 5t VILevi; 5c taylanozgurefe; 7cr Dmitry Kalinovsky; 7bl Aleksander Krsmanovic; 7br GIRODJL; 8-9 Markus Altmann; 9 Aleksander Krsmanovic; 10-11bg Surkov Dimitri; 10bl Gabriele Danesi; 11c Ververidis Vasilis; 11b vallefrias; 12t Budimir Jevtic, 12bl Vladimir Nenezic; 12br Zorandim; 13bl Vladimir Nenezic; 13br Aleksei Kolesnikov; 16-17bg Jocic; 16t MaZiKab; 16b Vadim Ratnikov; 17t Michaelpuche; 17c Stockr; 17b Horsemen; 19tr VILevi; 19tl Przemek Tokar; 19bl Maggee; 23t Frederico Rostagno; 23c © age fotostock; 23b VILevi, 24-25 Alex Yeung; 25tl Alexander Erdbeer; 25c Andriy Solovyov, 25bl Aisyaqilumar2; 25br Joe Gough; 26-27 Alexander Erdbeer; 27t Will Iredale; 28-29bg Frederic Legrand; 28t taylanozgurefe; 29t JFs Pic Factory; 29c Roman023; 29b Lisa S.; 30-31 brickrena; 31tr GIRODJL; 31tl Art Konovalov; 31bl VanderWolf Images; 31br TFoxFoto; 32-33 Dmitry Kalinovsky; 33t bogdanhoda; 34-35bg Anna Moskvina; 34t GIRODJL; 34b fstockfoto; GIRODJL; 35c TFoxFoto; 35b Horsemen; 36-37 Pavel L Photo and Video; 37tr Svaygert Ekaterina; 37cr Bram van Broekhoven; 37br Art Konovalov; 38-39 Blanscape; 39t TUM2282; 40t DyziO; 41t Aisyaqilumar2; 41c Large; 41b nitinut380; 42-43 Pavel L Photo and Video; 43t Dmitry Kalinovsky; 43cl Hellen Sergeyeva; 43cr Janet Faye Hastings; 43br alarich; 44-45 Tomislav Pinter; 45b Ari N; 46-47bg Hellen Sergeyeva; 46t Art Konovalov; 46b Albert Pego; 47t Fat Bird; 47c Chaiyapron Baokaew; 47b Dmitry Kalinovsky.

CONTENTS

BIG CONSTRUCTION MACHINES 4

AT THE QUARRY 6

MAKING A ROAD 12

DIGGING A TUNNEL 18

DEMOLITION TIME! 24

MOVING DIRT AND ROCKS 30

DIGGING FOUNDATIONS 36

BUILDING SKYSCRAPERS 42

ANSWERS 48

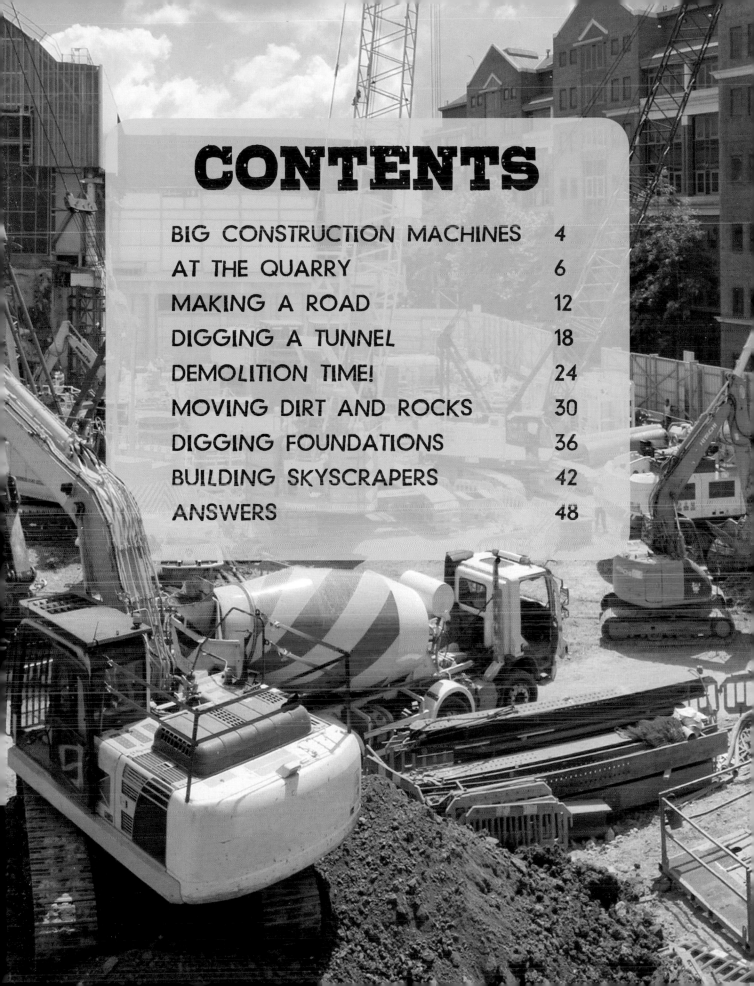

BIG CONSTRUCTION MACHINES

Welcome to the world of Big Machines! All of the big, tough machines in this book help us build stuff. They work on construction sites, demolition sites, and in quarries. They dig deep holes, break up enormous rocks, carry loads of soil, lift heavy building materials, and smash down old buildings.

Some machines are great at cutting, breaking, and carrying rocks.

A machine like this can make roads as flat as a pancake!

Can you guess what a huge drilling machine like this might be used for?

Smash! Bang! Machines can be used to knock buildings down as well as build them.

Every job needs a special machine. As you find out about each big construction job in this book, see if you can guess which machine is just the right one to get the job done!

AT THE QUARRY

You'll find plenty of big machines at a noisy, dusty rock quarry. Sharp cutting machines saw lumps of rock from the hillside. Other powerful machines pull, push, and lift the pieces of rock. Tough trucks carry the rock away to factories to be chopped and polished.

The rock is used to make all sorts of things, such as buildings, bridges, and roads. We need big, powerful machines to get rock from a quarry...

Which machines would you choose?

Backhoe cutter

Wheeled loader

Road roller

Rock excavator

Bulldozer

ROCK EXCAVATOR

Look at this excavator working in a quarry. With just a flick of its bucket, it topples over massive chunks of rock the size of cars. You wouldn't want to arm wrestle one of these!

The boom reaches high into the air.

The bucket has pointy teeth that bite into the rock.

These wide metal tracks keep the excavator from sinking down into the sticky mud. They clank and squeak when the excavator is on the move.

These rams work like your muscles. But they're much, much stronger.

A powerful engine makes the tracks go around. It also works the arm.

The boom has two parts connected together.

Driving an excavator is fun. You pull, push, and press levers, pedals, and buttons to make the excavator's tracks, body, and arm move.

TRACKED EXCAVATOR IN NUMBERS

- **WEIGHT:** 57 tons
- **BOOM LENGTH:** 36 feet
- **ENGINE SIZE:** 12 liters
- **TOP SPEED:** 3 miles per hour

ROCKY JOBS

Here are all the big quarry machines working hard at their jobs.

② TRACKED EXCAVATOR

When the wire cutter has chopped a chunk of rock, the excavator gives a shove with its bucket. Over topples the rock. Crash!

① DIAMOND WIRE CUTTER

This machine has a long loop of wire covered in diamonds. The diamonds are very hard and tough. The machine pulls the wire around and around. The wire slowly slices through the rock.

3 BACKHOE CUTTER

The block is too heavy to move! A backhoe cutter powers up its saw and gets to work chopping up the giant rock blocks.

4 WHEELED LOADER

A wheeled loader slides its giant metal prongs under a lump of rock and scoops it up. Don't drop that rock!

5 FLATBED TRUCK

Gently does it! Very carefully, the loader lowers the heavy blocks onto the back of a truck. Next stop: the factory!

MAKING A ROAD

Roads are made of gravel with tarmac on the top. Road builders use machines to spread earth, gravel, and tarmac. They also need really heavy machines to squash everything down!

Which of these big machines would you need to build a road?

Grader

Truck crane

Compactor

Paving machine

Tunneling loader

PAVING MACHINE

A paving machine is like a magic road maker! A truck tips a steaming hot mixture of tar, gravel, and sand into one end of a paving machine. The mixture is called asphalt (say 'as-falt'). The paver spreads the asphalt out as it moves along, leaving behind a beautifully flat road surface.

PAVER IN NUMBERS

WEIGHT: 13 tons

LENGTH: 20 feet

WIDTH: 26 feet

PAVING SPEED: 66 feet per minute

The asphalt is spread out underneath here. The paver smooths it out.

The driver sits on top of the paver. He steers and controls the paver's speed.

The new asphalt slowly cools down. When it is cool, the tar works like glue, holding the pieces of gravel together.

The paver moves slowly along on two wide tracks.

The hopper stores hot asphalt, ready to be used.

ROAD BUILDING JOBS

Here are all the different machines that build roads.

GRADER

This is a giant smoothing machine! The blade underneath smooths out dirt or gravel as the grader moves along. It leaves a perfectly flat surface for the new road.

2 COMPACTOR

This is a giant squashing machine! It has heavy wheels covered with teeth. It rolls slowly across the ground, squashing the dirt to make it really hard.

3 MILLING MACHINE

Sometimes old asphalt must be dug up and replaced. This milling machine chews up asphalt and spits out the pieces! The pieces go along a conveyor belt and into a truck.

4 PAVING MACHINE

The paving machine puts a layer of asphalt down on the ground. It puts a thick layer down first, then a thin, smooth layer on top.

5 ROAD ROLLER

Along comes a road roller. Its heavy metal rollers press the asphalt down to make it very smooth. It sprays water on the warm asphalt to keep the asphalt from sticking to its rollers.

DIGGING A TUNNEL

Big digging machines work underground to build tunnels for roads and railroads. Machines dig tunnels in different ways. Some drill holes for explosives that blast away the rock. Some grind away rock, and some carry rubble out of the tunnel.

Which of these big machines would you need for tunneling?

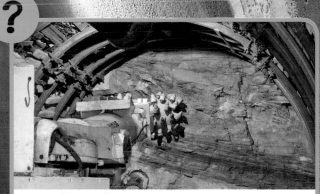

Roadheader

Tunnel-boring machine

Low-profile loader

Tracked excavator

Earth scraper

TUNNEL-BORING MACHINE

This amazing machine digs a tunnel all by itself. It's called a tunnel-boring machine, or TBM for short. It cuts through the rock, pushing itself along like a mole. As it moves, it builds a concrete lining in the tunnel behind it to keep the roof from falling in.

The cutting head is at the front of the machine. The head spins and the sharp teeth cut away the rock.

The shield is behind the cutting head. It keeps the tunnel roof and walls from falling down.

This cutting head has come out of the ground. It has finished digging its tunnel.

Rams push the cutting head forward.

A conveyor belt carries away all the loose pieces of rock from the cutting head.

A machine behind the shield puts up concrete panels to make the tunnel strong.

TUNNEL-BORING MACHINE IN NUMBERS

WEIGHT: 1,100 tons

LENGTH: 492 feet

WIDTH: 23 feet

CUTTING SPEED: 230 feet per day

TUNNELING JOBS

Here are all the different machines used to dig tunnels.

1 DRILLING JUMBO

This machine works in tunnels blasted by explosives. It drills lots of holes in the rock face. Explosives are pushed into the holes. Then... boom! The rock is blasted to pieces.

2 ROADHEADER

This machine digs away at the rock with a spinning cutting bit covered with sharp teeth. The bit moves from side to side and up and down to cut the rock.

3 LOW-PROFILE LOADER

Machines that work in tunnels can't be too tall! This low-profile loader can fit into fairly small tunnels. It scoops up all the pieces of rock blasted by explosives or dug out by drills.

4 TUNNEL TRUCK

Here's another low-profile machine. A loader fills it up with rock and rubble, which it carries away. It dumps the rock and rubble and comes back for more.

5 TUNNEL-BORING MACHINE

This huge machine does all the jobs of the other machines here, all by itself!

DEMOLITION TIME!

Some big machines knock things down instead of building them! They are demolition machines. They bash down old buildings and break the walls, floors, and roofs into tiny pieces. Then they take away all the waste that's left.

Which of these big machines would you need to demolish a building?

Demolition excavator

Wrecking ball

Concrete pump

Soil auger

Grapple

DEMOLITION EXCAVATOR

This big machine has giant jaws like a dinosaur! The jaws are called shears. They nibble away at concrete walls and floors, and rip down roofs. The long arm lets the shears reach high up to the upper floors of old buildings, so the excavator can pull them down.

The engine is under here.

The excavator moves around on its tough metal tracks. The tracks roll easily over rough ground and rubble.

The driver controls the tracks, the arm, and the shears with levers and pedals inside the cab.

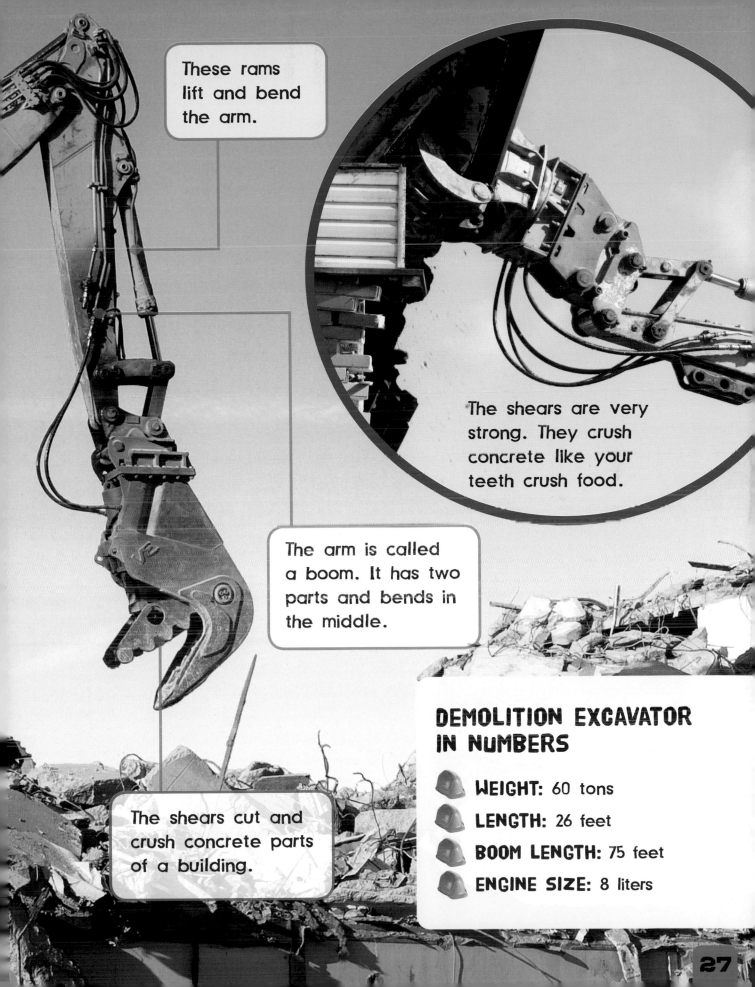

These rams lift and bend the arm.

The shears are very strong. They crush concrete like your teeth crush food.

The arm is called a boom. It has two parts and bends in the middle.

The shears cut and crush concrete parts of a building.

DEMOLITION EXCAVATOR IN NUMBERS

WEIGHT: 60 tons

LENGTH: 26 feet

BOOM LENGTH: 75 feet

ENGINE SIZE: 8 liters

DEMOLITION JOBS

Here are all the different machines that demolish buildings.

1 DEMOLITION EXCAVATOR

A demolition excavator uses its shears to bite off chunks of a building. The excavator also pulls and pushes the walls to knock them down. The rubble falls down to the ground.

2 WRECKING BALL

A crane swings a wrecking ball into the building. The heavy ball smashes off pieces of the building and knocks down the walls.

This is a powerful crunching machine. It fits on the end of an excavator's arm. The huge jaws crush lumps of concrete on the ground, turning them into rubble and dust.

④ CONCRETE BREAKER

Tough concrete is no match for this big machine. A concrete breaker is like a giant jackhammer. It hammers away at thick slabs of concrete to break them up.

⑤ GRAPPLE

A grapple or grab picks up pieces of metal and concrete like a grasping hand. The driver opens the grapple, drops it into the pile of waste, and closes it up to grab the waste.

MOVING DIRT AND ROCKS

Earth-moving machines are big machines that move dirt and rocks from one place to another. They dig, scrape, and scoop up dirt. They push it along, carry it around, and dump it where it's needed. They flatten the ground and build up banks of dirt, ready for buildings and roads.

Which of these big machines would you need to move dirt?

Bulldozer

Articulated hauler

Earth scraper

Grapple

Compactor

BULLDOZER

A bulldozer is a super-tough construction machine. It pushes heavy piles of dirt around with its huge metal blade. It also scrapes away soil, spreads it out, and pulls up tree stumps and boulders.

The driver controls the bulldozer from the cab.

This big claw tears up the ground. It is called a ripper.

The caterpillar tracks keep the bulldozer from sinking or slipping in gooey mud.

BULLDOZER IN NUMBERS

- **WEIGHT:** 55 tons
- **LENGTH:** 30 feet
- **BLADE WIDTH:** 10 feet
- **ENGINE SIZE:** 27 liters

Some bulldozers have more than one claw at the back.

The rams lift the blade up or push it down.

The bulldozer's powerful engine is under here.

The strong blade scrapes, pushes, and spreads dirt.

EARTH-MOVING JOBS

Here are all the different machines that move dirt on a building site.

1 EXCAVATOR

An excavator has a big bucket with sharp teeth. It scoops up bucketloads of dirt. Then it dumps it in a pile on the ground, or loads it onto the back of a truck.

2 EARTH SCRAPER

An earth scraper works like a giant vegetable slicer! As the scraper moves along, a wide blade scrapes away at the ground underneath. It stores the dirt in its hopper.

③ ARTICULATED HAULER

This tough truck can drive over rough, bumpy building sites. Its giant tires keep it from sinking into the mud, and give it a good grip. It is articulated, meaning that it bends in the middle.

④ DUMP TRUCK

A dump truck is a heavy truck that rumbles along, carrying dirt to or from a building site. The back tips up, and with a whoosh, all the dirt slides out.

⑤ BULLDOZER

A bulldozer pushes around the piles of dirt dug up by an excavator, or dropped by a dump truck.

DIGGING FOUNDATIONS

A building would topple over or sink into the ground if it had no foundations! Big, heavy buildings sit on long poles called piles. Some machines whack piles again and again to hammer them into the ground. Other machines dig deep holes for piles to go in, or mix concrete to use in the building's foundations.

Which of these big machines would you need to build foundations?

Paver

Auger

Concrete mixer

Piledriver

Articulated hauler

CONCRETE MIXER

This big machine is a concrete mixing truck. Sand, gravel, water, and cement are poured into its drum. Then the drum turns slowly as the truck drives along, mixing the ingredients to make concrete.

Water for the concrete comes from this tank.

The driver operates the truck from the cab.

Large wheels help the truck roll over rough ground.

CONCRETE MIXER IN NUMBERS

- **WEIGHT:** 6 tons
- **LENGTH:** 23 feet
- **AMOUNT OF CONCRETE:** 283 cubic feet

At the building site, the driver unfolds the delivery chute. The concrete comes out of the drum and down the chute.

The drum spins slowly, mixing up the concrete.

The ingredients for the concrete are poured into the hopper.

A strong frame called a chassis holds up the drum.

FOUNDATION JOBS

Here are all the powerful machines that build foundations.

1 AUGER

An auger makes holes, ready for concrete to be poured in to make piles. The auger has a giant screw that digs into the ground and pulls out the dirt.

2 PILEDRIVER

Crash! Bang! Smash! A piledriver hammers steel or concrete piles into the ground. It drops a heavy weight onto the top of the pile, smashing it into the ground.

③ PILE DRILL

A pile drill digs dirt from the ground with its bucket. It pushes the bucket into the ground and pulls it up full of dirt. The hole is then filled with concrete to make a pile.

④ BACKHOE LOADER

This handy machine digs long, narrow trenches in the ground. The trenches are filled with concrete to make strong foundations.

⑤ CONCRETE MIXER

A concrete mixer brings the concrete needed to make concrete piles. The delivery chute sends the concrete into holes made by augers and pile drills. The concrete makes a strong pile when it sets hard.

BUILDING SKYSCRAPERS

Skyscrapers are very tall buildings. Builders need big machines to construct them, and to build bridges and towers. Most of all, they need tall machines to lift all the pieces of the building, such as pieces of steel and buckets of concrete, high into the air.

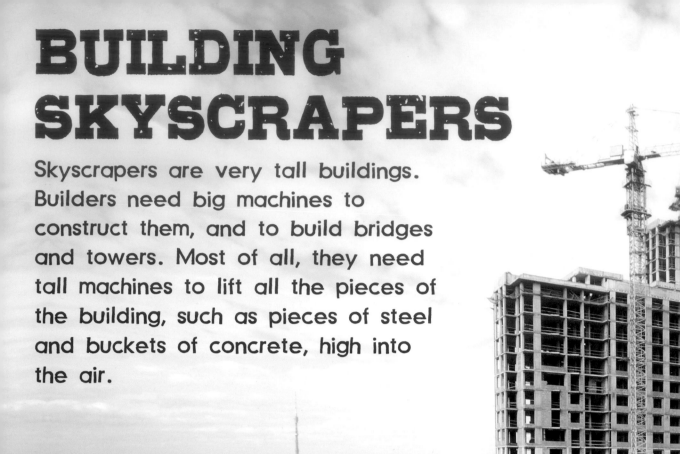

Which of these big machines would you need to build a skyscraper?

Concrete pump

Tower crane

Cherry picker

Pulverizer

Grader

TOWER CRANE

This is the tallest of all the big construction machines! A tower crane stands on the ground or on the top of a building, or sometimes it's attached to the side of a building. Extra pieces are added to make the crane bigger as a new building grows taller. Tower cranes look spindly, but they are very strong.

The counter jib is opposite the main jib. A heavy weight on the counter jib keeps the crane from toppling over when it's lifting heavy objects.

The trolley moves backward and forward along the main jib. The hook hangs from the trolley.

Things that the crane is going to lift are hung on the huge hook.

The tower that holds the crane up is called the mast. It is made of many sections joined together.

TOWER CRANE IN NUMBERS

- **MAXIMUM HEIGHT:** 360 feet
- **LENGTH OF BOOM:** 328 feet
- **BIGGEST WEIGHT IT CAN LIFT:** 110 tons

The main jib stretches out from the top of the mast.

Don't be a tower crane operator if you are scared of heights! The operator sits in a cab at the top of the mast.

SKYSCRAPER JOBS

Here are all the different machines that work hard to build skyscrapers.

1 TRUCK CRANE

A truck crane drives to the building site where it is needed. It picks up building materials from the ground and lifts them into place on the building.

2 CRAWLER CRANE

Clank, clank! A crawler crane moves around the building site on its huge metal tracks. Like the truck crane, it lifts building materials into the air.

3 TOWER CRANE

As a skyscraper gets taller and taller, a tower crane grows taller too. It lifts materials such as concrete up from the ground and drops them off at the top of the building.

4 CONCRETE PUMP

A concrete pump sucks concrete from a concrete mixer and pumps it along a pipe to where builders need it.

5 CHERRY PICKER

Up, up, and away! A cherry picker takes construction workers upward so they can connect the parts of a skyscraper together.

At the quarry (page 7)

Wheeled loader

Backhoe cutter

Rock excavator

Making a road (pages 12-13)

Grader

Compactor

Paving machine

Digging a tunnel (page 19)

Roadheader

Tunnel-boring machine

Low-profile loader

Demolition time! (page 25)

Demolition excavator

Wrecking ball

Grapple

Moving earth and soil (page 31)

Articulated hauler

Bulldozer

Earth scraper

Digging foundations (page 37)

Piledriver

Auger

Concrete mixer

Building skyscrapers (page 43)

Concrete pump

Tower crane

Cherry picker